Do You Like Saving Planet Earth?

T0102558

Diane Lindsey Reeves

Published in the United States of America by Cherry Lake Publishing Group
Ann Arbor, Michigan
www.cherrylakepublishing.com

Reading Adviser: Beth Walker Gambro, MS, Ed., Reading Consultant, Yorkville, IL

Photo Credits: cover: © Oakland Images/Shutterstock; page 5: © mervas/Shutterstock; page 6: © Tatevosian Yana/
Shutterstock; page 7: © YAKOBCHUK VIACHESLAV/Shutterstock; page 8: © fizkes/Shutterstock; page 9: © Rawpixel.com/
Shutterstock; page 10: © Maridav/Shutterstock; page 11: © TOM.RUETHAI/Shutterstock; page 12: © kryvoshapka/
Shutterstock; page 13: © boonchoke/Shutterstock; page 14: © rakratchada/Shutterstock; page 15: © Phovoir/
Shutterstock; page 16: © kittirat roekburi/Shutterstock; page 17: © PRESSLAB/Shutterstock; page 18: Katherine
Kendrick/USGS; page 19: Hawaiian Volcano Observatory/USGS; page 20: Kristi Rugg/NPS Photo; page 21: Catoctin
Mountain Park/NPS Photo; page 22: Suzanna Soileau/USGS; page 23: © Frame Stock Footage/Shutterstock; page 24:
© Avatar_023/Shutterstock; page 25: © gameanna/Shutterstock; page 26: © Bannafarsai_Stock/Shutterstock; page 27:
© Ingo Bartussek/Shutterstock; page 30: © Dmytro Zinkevych/Shutterstock; page 31: © Monkey Business Images/
Shutterstock

Copyright © 2023 by Cherry Lake Publishing Group

All rights reserved. No part of this book may be reproduced or utilized in any form or by any means without written
permission from the publisher.

Cherry Lake Press is an imprint of Cherry Lake Publishing Group.

Library of Congress Cataloging-in-Publication Data has been filed and is available at catalog.loc.gov

Cherry Lake Publishing Group would like to acknowledge the work of the Partnership for 21st Century Learning,
a Network of Battelle for Kids. Please visit *http://www.battelleforkids.org/networks/p21* for more information.

Printed in the United States of America
Corporate Graphics

Diane Lindsey Reeves likes to write books that help students figure out what they want
to be when they grow up. She mostly lives in Washington, D.C., but spends as much time
as she can in North Carolina and South Carolina with her grandkids.

CONTENTS

Going Green with a Cool Career

Figuring out what you want to be when you grow up can be tricky. There are so many choices! How are you supposed to know which one to pick? Here's an idea... follow the clues!

The fact that you are reading a book called *Do You Like Saving Planet Earth?* is your first clue. It suggests that you have an interest in the environment. True? If so, start looking at different careers where you can sustain a cool future!

Your **interests** say a lot about who you are and what makes you tick. What do you like doing best?

Abilities are things that you are naturally good at doing. Another word for ability is talent. Everyone has natural talents and abilities. Some are more obvious than others. What are you really good at doing?

Curiosity offers up other career clues. To succeed in any career, you have to learn what it takes to do that job. You may have to go to college or trade school. It may take gaining new skills and getting experience. Curiosity about a subject keeps you at it until you learn what you need to know. What do you want to know more about?

Interests. Abilities. Curiosity. These clues can help you find a career that's right for you.

FIND THE CLUES!

Each chapter includes several clues about careers you might enjoy.

INTERESTS: What do you like doing?

ABILITIES: What are you good at doing?

CURIOSITY: What do you want to learn more about?

Are You a Future Tree Hugger?

WOULD YOU ENJOY...

Being the boss of all things green at a company?
(see page 8)

Leading tours that celebrate the best of nature?
(see page 10)

Solving problems to protect the environment?
(see page 12)

Finding new ways to keep the world clean? (see page 14)

Tackling big issues with science and math? (see page 16)

Making better use of the world's fossil fuels? (see page 18)

Working in the great outdoors? (see page 20)

Keeping an eye on the weather? (see page 22)

Helping the world quench its thirst? (see page 24)

Making energy in windy ways? (see page 26)

READ ON FOR MORE CLUES ABOUT EARTH-FRIENDLY CAREERS!

Chief Sustainability Officer

A person who is in charge of environmental programs at a company.

Big corporations use lots of **natural resources** and create lots of waste. Sometimes their processes cause pollution and other problems. Someone must make sure they make things right. Enter the chief **sustainability** officers! Their job is to come up with smarter ways to do business. They look for ways to get the job done with less harm to the environment. This includes preventing pollution and starting recycling programs. It's all about being good corporate citizens.

CLUES!

INTEREST: Getting involved in environmental projects

ABILITY: Thinking creatively and solving problems

CURIOSITY: Ways big business can go green

INVESTIGATE!

NOW: Suggest ways your school can save energy and recycle more.

LATER: Earn a college degree in business administration or sustainability studies.

Eco Tour Guide

A person who leads tours to natural areas where conservation is practiced and respected.

Would you like to visit a rain forest in Costa Rica? How about a safari to see giraffes, lions, and rhinos in Kenya? Or stay closer to home and lead tours to **eco-friendly** farms? These types of tours are part adventure and part education. Eco tour guides show tourists how to do things that they don't normally do. They must be responsible leaders. They also educate tourists about the history and science of their tour destination. Their goal is to get people close to nature and show them how to protect and preserve it. Most of all, eco tour guides love fun adventures!

CLUES!

INTEREST: Checking out interesting tourist sites

ABILITY: Being daring and adventurous

CURIOSITY: How to connect people with nature in fun ways

INVESTIGATE!

NOW: Take your friends on an eco tour of your neighborhood.

LATER: College is not required, but science knowledge is necessary.

Ecologist

A person who studies the relationship between living things and their habitats.

Ecologists are scientists who ask a lot of questions about the environment. How will building new houses affect local wildlife? Why is a species going extinct? How does air and water pollution affect humans? They study all life forms—from the tiny **nanobe** to the gigantic blue whale. They research **ecosystems** and make discoveries that save lives and protect nature. Ecologists conduct research outside where they make observations and collect samples. They work inside to make sense of the data. Ecologists write reports to share their answers with the rest of the world.

CLUES!

INTEREST: Exploring things you find in nature

ABILITY: Digging deep to learn new things

CURIOSITY: Finding new ways to explain how the environment works

INVESTIGATE!

NOW: Ask environmental questions and look for answers.

LATER: Earn a college degree in biology, ecology, or environmental science.

Energy Auditor

A person who looks for ways a business or home can save energy.

Energy auditors give good energy advice. These experts know a lot about construction, electrical systems, and energy. They go onsite to businesses and homes to see how clients can use less energy. They use special tools like **thermal infrared cameras** and blower-door tests to find energy leaks. They conduct hands-on tests on heating and cooling systems. Inspections can take auditors from basement boiler rooms all the way to rooftops. Auditors give clients ideas for how to use energy more efficiently. The best part of this job? Saving energy while helping clients save money on energy bills!

CLUES!

INTEREST: Investigating mysteries

ABILITY: Giving advice to friends

CURIOSITY: How people use energy at home and work

INVESTIGATE!

NOW: Look for ways your family can use less electricity at home.

LATER: Earn a 2- or 4-year college degree in mechanical engineering or environmental science and a certification.

Environmental Engineer

A person who develops solutions to environmental problems.

Environmental engineers are problem solvers. The quality of air, water, and soil are big issues for them. Recycling, waste disposal, and pollution get their attention. As the world population passes 8 billion people, they look for ways to make sure people everywhere have clean water and food. The first known environmental engineer was a man named Joseph Bazalgette. He designed an elaborate sewer system in London. This was in the mid-1800s when people were dying of **cholera** because of unclean water supplies. His sewer solution saved countless lives and lots of stink! What will environmental engineers think of next?

CLUES!

INTEREST: Wondering how things work

ABILITY: Taking things apart and putting them back together again

CURIOSITY: Using math and science to solve environmental problems

INVESTIGATE!

NOW: Get involved in all the STEM activities you can.

LATER: Earn a college degree in civil or environmental engineering.

Geologist

A person who studies rocks and the natural processes associated with rocks.

There's more to rocks than meets the eye! Rocks are involved in earthquakes, volcanos, and climate change. Rocks are home to precious gems and minerals. Some rocks, called fossils, even tell stories about Earth's history. The oil and gasoline that provide energy for modern life are found deep within Earth's rocky surface. Geologists pick their favorite types of rocks to study. There are environmental geologists, marine geologists, petroleum geologists, and more. They work in the field, in labs, and with technology. It's all in a day's work for smart, curious geologists. Go rocks!

CLUES!

INTEREST: Collecting different kinds of rocks

ABILITY: Discovering something new every day

CURIOSITY: Uncovering Earth's story with rocks

INVESTIGATE!

NOW: Take all the science and math classes you can.

LATER: Earn a college degree in geology.

Park Ranger

A person who manages and protects national and state parks.

What do the Grand Canyon, Yosemite, and Yellowstone all have in common? They are all beautiful national parks! Park rangers work in places like these in state and national parks all over the country. Job number one is protecting the land and the wildlife. They do this in so many ways. Fire prevention is high on their to-do lists. They maintain trails and keep track of the animal population. They interact with plenty of humans, too. Park rangers educate guests about nature and search for them when they get lost. They get serious about enforcing laws about hunting and **arson**.

CLUES!

INTEREST: Enjoying the great outdoors

ABILITY: Telling other people about nature

CURIOSITY: Natural habitats of wildlife

INVESTIGATE!

NOW: Visit as many state and national parks as you can.

LATER: Get park ranger law enforcement training.

Meteorologist

A person who forecasts the weather.

Meteorologists predict the future, but not with crystal balls. They use high-tech equipment like Doppler radar and weather satellites. Technology helps them forecast what weather will be like today, tomorrow, and beyond. Some meteorologists share their forecasts on radio, TV, and online news. Most meteorologists work behind the scenes. They do research and study data to increase the accuracy of forecasts and weather warnings that keep people safe. The federal government employs the most meteorologists. They work for an agency called the National Oceanic and Atmospheric Administration (NOAA).

CLUES!

INTEREST: Keeping tabs on the weather

ABILITY: Knowing how to be prepared in all types of weather

CURIOSITY: The effects of climate change on weather

INVESTIGATE!

NOW: Keep a weather log and see how your predictions match reality.

LATER: Earn a college degree in meteorology or atmospheric science.

Water Treatment Specialist

A person who makes sure a community's water supply is safe to use.

Thirsty? Thanks to water treatment specialists, refreshing, clean water is as close as your kitchen sink. Communities everywhere rely on these professionals to keep water supplies safe and clean. Water treatment specialists work at water or sewer treatment plants and factories. Cleaning water is complicated. It involves massive systems of pipes, drains, and equipment. Most public water systems follow five important steps that include **filtration** and **disinfection**. There are many rules about doing it right. Water treatment specialists need to know a lot about chemistry and biology to keep water supplies safe.

CLUES!

INTERESTS: Studying the water cycle, chemistry, biology, and data

ABILITIES: Having strong problem-solving skills

CURIOSITY: Helping keep other people safe and healthy

INVESTIGATE!

NOW: Figure out where water from your house goes to get clean.

LATER: Earn a college degree in chemistry, biology, or civil engineering.

Wind Turbine Technician

A person who installs, inspects, maintains, operates, and repairs wind turbines.

A wind turbine is a cool device that turns wind into electrical energy. Wind turbine technicians, or wind techs, install and maintain these devices on wind farms. These wind farms provide clean energy for manufacturing companies and communities. The job requires technical skill and physical stamina. Duties include monitoring turbines from the ground and climbing towers for inspections and repair. Wind turbine towers are almost as tall as the Statue of Liberty! Wind is seen as an exciting alternative fuel source. Wind is clean, it's free, and there is an endless supply of it.

CLUES!

INTERESTS: Finding alternative energy sources

ABILITIES: Keeping active and learning by doing

CURIOSITY: Finding better ways to energize the world

INVESTIGATE!

NOW: Go online to find instructions for building a mini wind turbine.

LATER: Earn a degree from a technical school and get on-the-job training.

Planet Earth Workshop

Keep investigating those career clues until you find a career that's right for you! Here are more ways to explore.

Join a Club

Talk to your parents or teachers about starting a Kids Eco Club.
Find more information at: http://www.kidsecoclub.org

Talk to People with Interesting Careers

Ask your teacher or parent to help you connect with someone who has a career like the one you want.
Be ready to ask lots of questions!

Volunteer

Celebrate Earth Day on April 22 by helping clean up your community. For that matter, look for ways to pitch in and help all year long!

Enjoy Career Day

School career days can be a great way to find out more about different careers. Make the most of this opportunity.

Explore Online

With adult supervision, use your favorite search engine to look online for information about careers you are interested in.

Participate in Take Your Daughters and Sons to Work Day

Every year on the fourth Thursday of April, kids all over the world go to work with their parents or other trusted adults to find out what the world of work is really like.

Find out more at: https://daughtersandsonstowork.org

Resources

Chief Sustainability Officer
YouTube: Chief Sustainability Officers Career Video
https://www.youtube.com/watch?v=KHi_Vns5gc4

Eco Adventure Guide
YouTube: Eco-Adventures
https://www.youtube.com/watch?v=al-do-HGuIk

Ecologist
YouTube: Ecology for Kids
https://www.youtube.com/watch?v=YCw8pGbx2dg

Energy Auditor
The Nature Conservancy: Calculate Your Carbon Footprint
https://www.nature.org/en-us/get-involved/how-to-help/carbon-footprint-calculator

Environmental Engineer
EPA: Science Fair Environmental Project Ideas
https://www.epa.gov/students/science-fair-environmental-project-ideas

Geologist
OneGeology Kids
https://www.onegeology.org/eXtra/kids/english/home.html

Park Ranger
National Park Service: Become a Junior Ranger
https://www.nps.gov/kids/become-a-junior-ranger.htm

Meteorologist
Drimmer, Stephanie Warren. *Ultimate Weatherpedia.*
Washington, DC: National Geographic Kids, 2019.

Water Treatment Specialist
YouTube: Water and You
https://www.youtube.com/watch?v=tuYB8nMFxQA

Wind Turbine Technician
YouTube: How is Wind Energy Produced?
https://www.youtube.com/watch?v=-8-9j3mXIYE

Glossary

abilities (uh-BIH-luh-teez) natural talents or acquired skills

arson (AR-suhn) crime of setting fire to a property on purpose

cholera (KAH-luh-ruh) dangerous disease caused by contaminated water

curiosity (kyur-ee-AH-suh-tee) strong desire to know or learn about something

disinfection (dis-in-FEK-shuhn) process used to kill germs

eco-friendly (ee-koh-FREND-lee) opposite of environmentally harmful

ecosystem (EE-koh-sih-stuhm) all the living things in a place

filtration (fil-TRAY-shuhn) process of removing small particles from water

interests (IN-tuh-ruhsts) things or activities that a person enjoys or is concerned about

nanobe (nah-NOHB) tiny filamental structure first found in some rocks and sediments; scientists believe it to be one of the smallest life forms on Earth

natural resources (NAH-chuh-ruhl REE-sohr-suhz) raw materials from nature that can be used for economic gain

sustainability (suh-stay-nuh-BIH-luh-tee) meeting current needs without compromising future needs

thermal infrared cameras (THUHR-muhl in-fruh-RED KAM-ruhs) devices that create images using infrared radiation

Index